HORSE-SCENTS

or

A Tale of Chip and Patty's Perfume Emporium, Rooming House, and Manure Museum

The Dashing Western Romance of a Cowgal
—and her Cowguy (sort-of)
—and his Mammal

A Play-Within-A-Movie-Within-A-Play

Concept, Dialogue, Attitude, and Every Other Dang Thing
by
J MICK DUNNA

Dramatic Publishing
Woodstock, Illinois • London, England • Melbourne, Australia

Printed in the United States of America

(HORSE-SCENTS)

Cover design by Susan Carle

ISBN 0-87129-561-X

To Allen Shankles, Jim Kemp,
and the Amarillo Little Theatre Board of Directors;
to Bobby and Mary Ann Lee,
and, most especially, to the original cast and company:

Cindi Bradley, Michael Bradley, Christi Campbell,
Shad Campbell, Sam H. Childers, Marnie Dodson,
Brent McFarland, David McGinnis, Don Shipman,
Amy Sloger, Christy Smith, Amy Gililland,
Patrick Lippincott, Amber Palmer, J Mick Dunna,
Loren Strickland, and Production Director Carl Cox

HORSE-SCENTS was first produced by Amarillo Little Theatre in The Playhouse at The Big Texan Steak Ranch, Amarillo, Texas.

A Note From The Author

HORSE-SCENTS, as does any melodrama, depends upon the unkindness of strangers. (Sorry, Mr. Williams.) Villainesses, villains, bad jokes, stupid stunts, idiotic behavior, and anything else that strikes the audience as moronic is equally booed, hissed, and made into a popcorn target. All attempts at keeping order during *HORSE-SCENTS* are doomed to failure—and will probably yield perpetrator-specific booing, hissing, and popcorn targeting.

Here are a few well-thought-out hints, drawn from experience:

1. Always use dry, unsalted popcorn—NEVER BUTTERED!

2. Remove the popcorn from the can or box BEFORE distributing (or SELLING) it to the audience.

3. Sweep up the corn immediately after the show and DO NOT RE-USE IT!—some people actually eat this stuff! (And spare me your snotty letters about the values of recycling—where do you think most melodrama jokes come from?)

There is only one rule in the production of HORSE-SCENTS—If you're not having fun, re-examine what you have been doing. The play is nothing. I mean, the play is nothing if it is not fun—fun for the audience AND for the cast.

May you be perpetually in the chips.

Fragrantly,
J Mick Dunna

HORSE-SCENTS

A Comic Melodrama in Two Acts
For 6 men, 4 women, 4 double-able minor roles, extras

RIDICULIS PERSONAE

Featured Roles

C.B.* .... pushy Director of HORSE-SCENTS—The Movie
TOAD** ....assistant to C.B. (Universal Double)
CHIP ....chef and internationally recognized manure fancier
PATTY ....perfume designer and mystic groupie
SWEET ROADY ....their sweet, innocent, but determinedly self-sufficient daughter
VANCE LANCELOT ....our mysterious hero
SPUD .... Vance's devoted, mysterious sidekick
ARNOLD ... Manure Museum curator, accomplice of Avaricia, secret admirer of Roady
AVARICIA SLIME .... President and sensuous C.E.O. (Congenitally Evil Officer) of Vendetta Savings and Loan
DEBIT .. Avaricia's clueless, yet undeniably sexy henchwoman

Ensemble Roles

PARVO** .... a dog—really a person—how can you depend on a dog? (usually played by TOAD)
FLIGGER .... offstage "voice" of the Dolphin
WOMAN-WHO-FIXES-OW-OWS** ......healer, one with nature, lost with almost everything else (usually played by TOAD)
PLUGHORSE STRAINS** ....sensational(izing) lawyer (usually played by TOAD)

Cheap Labor Roles

*EXTRAS, BIT PLAYERS, LOW-IMPACT STUNT PERSONS, BANK DRUDGES, DOG INTERPRETERS, SHARK CHOIR, FILM DIRECTOR IMPERSONATORS, SEA CREATURES AND WHO KNOWS WHAT ELSE—Played by Audience Members

* Roles which may be double- or multiple-cast

**Roles which are non-gender-specific, which can be done in drag, or which just don't care one way or the other

LOCALE

Chip and Patty's Perfume Emporium,
Rooming House, and Manure Museum
in Plop, Texas,
just off the trail.

SCENE

Mostly in Chip and Patty's lobby,
but at a couple of other nifty places, too.

TIME

Before anything really handy had been invented.
1893, say.
There may be a FEW anachronisms.

HORSE-SCENTS

AT RISE: *The lobby of Chip and Patty's Perfume Emporium, Rooming House, and Manure Museum. Before the play begins, a few announcements are made by C.B. SeVille's assistant and power yes-man, TOAD.*

TOAD *(stepping onto the stage)*. Ladies and Gentlemen, the making of photos or videos is prohibited during HORSE-SCENTS. The cast insists that there be no physical evidence of their—uh—performance. Now *(Gesturing grandly toward the door.)*...your director, Mr. C.B. SeVille.

(From an outside entrance, perhaps at the back of the house, C.B. SEVILLE enters. He is the classic film director—beret, scarf, silk shirt, puttees, riding boots, and riding crop or swagger stick.)

C.B. *(flamboyantly—a rather pushy person)*. Coming through, people! Com-ing through! Make way for your fabulously gifted film-maker! *(Proceeds to the stage. Looks over the crowd.)* Splendid extras, eh, Toad?

TOAD. Splendid.

C.B. *(aside, stage whisper to TOAD, while still smiling at the crowd)*. What whacko bin did they dig this mob out of?

TOAD. Splendid, B.O.

C.B. *(correcting)*. C.B.!

TOAD *(memorizing by rote)*. C.B., C.B., C.B...

C.B. *(to audience).* In my film, you play the audience at a western melodrama, among other things. Our location is Chip and Patty's Perfume Emporium, Rooming House, and Manure Museum—also known as "The Poopera House."

TOAD *(coaching audience).* Picture it in your minds. Or—just look at the stage.

C.B. Now, for your acting *(Speaking that most powerful of words.)* "motivation." You will "Boo" and "Hiss" the villainess, Avaricia Slime, C.E.O. of Vendetta Savings and Loan, and her assistant, Debit.

TOAD *(calling through megaphone, uncomfortably near C.B.'s ear).* Slime and Debit to the set!

(AVARICIA enters from her "office" as C.B. continues. DEBIT trails behind her.)

C.B. Booing rehearsal! And hissing. And popcorn throwing.

AVARICIA *(with incredibly forced malice).* You'll be booing out of the other side of your pocketbooks when I foreclose on Chip and Patty—when the Perfume Emporium, the Rooming House, AND, unfortunately, the Manure Museum, become mine!

DEBIT *(stupidly—always).* Hers!

AVARICIA *(to audience in general).* Every one of you will be—unemployed! *(Hideous laughter.)*

DEBIT *(stupidly—see above).* Unemployed! Tee-hee!

C.B. Maxi-booing, people! Mega-hissing! A panorama of popcorn!

AVARICIA *(among enormous boos, hisses, and popcorn).* You'll regret this, my pretties. And your little dog, too!

DEBIT. They got a dog named "Too"?

AVARICIA *(dragging DEBIT out).* Let's get out of here.

DEBIT. Can I see the doggy first?

AVARICIA. Out! *(They exit, DEBIT pausing briefly to wave to C.B. and blow him a kiss. [He obviously wishes this kept quiet and gestures her out.] During lulls in her role, DEBIT flirts with audience members indiscriminately—without stealing focus, naturally.)*

C.B. *(back on track).* You should also save some boos for…

TOAD. Who's the drunk?

C.B. Drunk?

TOAD. The one you're saving booze for.

C.B. *(explaining as if to a very slow child).* I mean that there is ANOTHER villain—the Manure Museum Curator, Arnold Benedict.

TOAD *(impressed).* Whoa—high budget.

(ARNOLD appears in the museum door, carrying a tray of cow chips—props only, please! Major booing and hissing.)

ARNOLD. Let Avaricia have the real estate. My lust is for—the livestock! Particularly that most precious petal in the population of Plop—Sweet Roady! *(Audience boos him unmercifully. Dropping character and holding up a cow chip, directly to audience.)* Hey, if you had my working conditions, you'd turn out bad, too. *(He exits, to a crush of verbal derision and popped disapproval.)*

C.B. On to more pleasant vistas. *(To audience.)* Our hero is the valiant Vance Lancelot. Vance should be cheered with shameless abandon.

(VANCE steps boldly onto the set through the DL doorway, smiling nobly.)

VANCE. Howdy, buckaroos. *(Audience, abandoning shame, cheers.)*

C.B. Less abandon! More shame! *(Audience does so.)* Thank you, Vance. *(VANCE is still standing nobly.)* That's it, boy. *(No VANCE response.)* Scram, moron! *(VANCE, never losing his smile, touches the brim of his hat in farewell, and exits.)*

TOAD. Superb directing, B.M.

C.B. *(hits TOAD, then continues).* Finally—we heave a collective sigh for the beauty, the innocence, the pure Western moxie of—sweet Roady.

(Sweet ROADY enters, nay, floats onto the stage, from the U doorway, accompanied by collective sighing-like-crazy from the audience.)

C.B. Big sigh!

ROADY. Good morrow, fair friends. *(As she exits, she kind of shudders, as if to say, "Geesh, what a wuss of a character.")*

TOAD *(to audience).* Sigh like that every time she comes on. Or until you get sick of it.

C.B. All is prepared, Toad—you may intone the sacred phrase.

TOAD *(to audience).* I have ALWAYS wanted to say this—*(With attitude, megaphone.)* Ready when you are, C.B. *(C.B. starts to hit him, then realizes he finally got it right.)*

C.B. *(moving to a position from which he can observe the play).* ACTION!

(CHIP rushes on from U, carrying a large pot of something which he places on the front desk as he speaks.)

CHIP. Patty! I nearly have it perfected.

(PATTY enters and crosses to him, speaking.)

PATTY. You think so, Chip?

CHIP *(pointing into the pot)*. Finally, the right combination of spaghetti, rigatoni, macaroni, linguini, and apples.

PATTY. Mackintosh apples or golden delicious?

CHIP. No, my favorite kind—road apples.

PATTY. Yum. My new perfume's about ripe, too. *(Sprays an atomizer into the air.)* It just needs a few more road apples, if you can spare them.

CHIP. We'll have to gather a new batch.

(Their lovely daughter, ROADY, has entered, looking quite disconsolate.)

CHIP. 'Morning, Roady.

ROADY *(distractedly)*. ...Pa.

PATTY. You look poorly, girl.

ROADY. Oh, it's nothing. I just wanted to think...and to write. *(Stands behind the front desk and opens a notebook. Writing.)* "Dear Dairy..."

CHIP *(to PATTY)*. Doesn't she mean, "Diary"?

PATTY. No, it's a letter to those cows she met at the Cottage Cheese Extravaganza and Barn Dance last year. What an animal lover.

CHIP. That's for sure. Who else would let that mangy dog of hers live?

PATTY. Parvo is not mangy.

CHIP. He needs a new groomer, then, 'cause somethin's makin' him butt-ugly.

ROADY *(writing)*. Things get worse and worse here at home...

CHIP. If she's just thinking and writing, how can we hear her?

PATTY. It's a stage device.

CHIP. Great! There hasn't been a stage through here since forever.

PATTY. Not that kind of stage, you ignoramus.

CHIP. Don't make fun of a man's religion, Patty. *(Both turn back to their work.)*

C.B. *(to TOAD)*. Prepare Parvo for his entrance.

TOAD. Uh, he didn't show up yet.

C.B. Then you know what to do.

TOAD. No!

C.B. It keeps costs down.

TOAD *(kneeling, begging)*. Don't make me play the dog again, please!

C.B. *(pointing his finger)*. Report to costuming. *(TOAD exits, noisily grumbling something deeply obscene which cannot be understood—thank heavens.)*

CHIP. Time to prove the pudding. *(Dips his finger into the pot, then licks the finger.)* Definitely needs more apples.

PATTY *(sprays the atomizer into the air, then walks through the mist. Inhales deeply)*. Mine needs them, too.

CHIP. To the foo-foo fields! *(He takes a highly-decorated, Easter-style basket from the front desk and heads for the front door.)*

PATTY. Can't we just grab some out of the Poopera House?

CHIP *(stops, turns, aghast)*. And destroy my perfect collection?! Every trail-twinky has a personality of its own, Patty!

PATTY. They are cow chips, Chip.

CHIP. And horse-chips! And pig-chips! And don't forget my luscious little lamb-chips. Each pasture-pumpkin is like my own child.

PATTY. I CAN see the resemblance.

CHIP. Let's go—the bovine-biscuits await. It's too noisy in here, anyway.

PATTY *(grabbing her own decorated basket).* Yeah, those stage devices make an awful racket.

CHIP *(calling to their sole employee).* Arnold, you keep an eye on things in the museum.

(They exit to outside, L, as ARNOLD enters from R, speaking in his faux-subservient mode.)

ARNOLD. Certainly, Mr. Chip. *(Aside to audience, dropping subservience.)* Like we're gonna have shoplifters. *(Notices ROADY. Nearly swoons.)* Ah! It is she! Sweet Roady, apple of my eye. She must be mine! Arrangements—hee, hee—WILL be made!

ROADY. Arnold—I didn't hear you come in.

ARNOLD *(subservient attitude again).* Forgive me for disturbing you, Miss Roady. I shall return to my rightful place among the cattle-cakes.

ROADY. You shouldn't put yourself down that way, Arnold.

ARNOLD. You mean—you actually think well of me?

ROADY. Certainly not. But put yourself down a different way. I'm sick of that one.

ARNOLD. How about, "I go—to submerge my wretched self in bull-binkies."

ROADY *(critiquing).* Fresh, AND aromatic.

ARNOLD. Oh, thank you. *(To audience, a pathetic attempt at macho.)* She wants me. *(He exits.)*

(TOAD re-enters in a cheap, cheap, cheap dog costume.)

ROADY. Parvo! Jump up here, boy. *(TOAD, humiliated and still mumble-cursing, climbs grudgingly onto the desk near her and adopts a semi-doggy pose. ROADY resumes her writing. PARVO serves as a kind of silent commentator—reacting to the stupidity of her letter as she writes.)* Where was I? "Dear Dairy. I don't know what we are to do, my four-stomached friends. There have been no customers for the rooming house or MaMAH's Perfume Emporium in many moons. Maybe if we could get all the mooning stopped...*(Sighs.)* Daddy's Manure Museum is—oh, he said to thank you for remembering him at Christmas—the museum is doing the same as ever. But our first visitor should arrive any year now. Ma hopes to land a contract with the Phoenix Fragrance Foundation and Daddy applied for a National Endowment for the Fertilization Arts grant, but so far no word from either place. We aren't starving, but I can't remember the last time we had a nice steak or a meatloaf or even a lousy hamburger and..." *(PARVO has snapped his head up and grabbed ROADY's pen. He looks at ROADY disapprovingly, shakes his head, takes the pen and scratches out the last paragraph. He returns the pen to her. ROADY, realizing, pats PARVO's funky head.)* Good thinking, boy. *(She recommences writing.)* "Did I tell you we have become vegetarians? We're just waiting to get a minister so we can begin holding services. Have to close now. Warm-handedly, Roady." *(She folds the letter carefully, then pulls a large box full of papers from beneath the desk and throws the freshly-written page in.)* If we ever get mail service, I'm gonna have SOME postage bill, huh, Parvo?

(PARVO rolls his eyes, disgusted. ROADY sighs very loudly and exits, U. The sigh has rolled PARVO off the

counter and he disappears behind it. AVARICIA's evil, wicked, heart-stopping, hammy laugh is heard. She enters, through the audience, shadowed by DEBIT.)

C.B. Boos! Hisses! Exploded kernels!

AVARICIA *(after menacing the audience, laughing evilly. To DEBIT)*. No mail service, eh? Ha, ha! Ha, ha!

DEBIT *(laughing very stupidly, actually pronouncing the word "ha")*. Ha ha. Ha ha. No mail service. Ha ha. Ha ha. Uh, boss?

AVARICIA. What?

DEBIT. What's so funny about not having mail service?

AVARICIA. Because, Debit, we know WHY they don't have mail service.

DEBIT. Oh. *(Nodding.)* Ha ha. Ha ha. *(Stopping.)* Why?

AVARICIA. Because we are intercepting their mail service, idiot!

DEBIT *(thinks briefly, how else, then:)*. What's the mail service idiot's name?

AVARICIA *(wearily, sarcastically)*. Debit.

DEBIT. Hey! Same as mine! I wonder if we're twins.

AVARICIA. Come on. We have to meet my secret accomplice.

DEBIT. He's ashamed of his piano playing?

AVARICIA. Not accompanist, ACCOMPLICE!

DEBIT. Oh. *(She opens her mouth to say something else, then realizes that she doesn't know anything else. During this, AVARICIA has moved onto the set. She hisses in the direction of the museum.)*

AVARICIA. Hsssst! Hsssst!

DEBIT *(who has not been paying very close attention—she can't)*. SNAKE! *(She slams AVARICIA with her hat, re-*

peatedly. Slows down the hitting when AVARICIA looks up at her. She has nearly stopped when AVARICIA speaks.)

AVARICIA. Debit. Come closer.

DEBIT *(holding her hat in front of her)*. Not that, boss.

AVARICIA. Closer.

DEBIT. I'll shut up. I'll be good.

AVARICIA. Closer. *(DEBIT resigns herself and puts her face close to AVARICIA's. AVARICIA, very deliberately and fully open to the audience, reaches into DEBIT's nostril and yanks out a hair. DEBIT reacts extremely visibly.)*

DEBIT. Oooh, I hate that.

AVARICIA *(to audience)*. It's called aversion therapy.

DEBIT. I thought it was called a nose hair.

AVARICIA. Shut up! *(She turns back toward the museum.)* Hsssst!

(DEBIT pulls off her hat and yells "SNA... " but AVARICIA has whipped around and is holding her nose-hair-pulling fingernails toward DEBIT. DEBIT replaces her hat as ARNOLD enters, skulkily.)

ARNOLD. I told you never to come here.

AVARICIA. Are you kidding? It's the only set this show has.

ARNOLD. Never mind. What do you want?

AVARICIA. Have you intercepted all of their mail?

ARNOLD. Yes. And you've got to act fast, Avaricia. The perfume deal AND the fertilizer grant both came through. *(Showing two letters.)* These are the confirmation letters.

AVARICIA *(taking the letters)*. I'll foreclose on Chip and Patty immediately.

DEBIT *(reflecting)*. Immediately. I never knew their last name before.

ARNOLD *(ignoring DEBIT's stupidity)*. After the foreclosure, sweet Roady will be mine.

AVARICIA. And I'll land that steaming chunk of muscular manhood—Chip.

DEBIT. How does that work?

AVARICIA. They'll be penniless. It's either accept us—or starve!

DEBIT. What about Patty?

AVARICIA. You can have her.

DEBIT. Typical. *(Indicating each person.)* He gets the girl. She gets the guy. I get the Patty.

AVARICIA *(to ARNOLD)*. I'll draw up the eviction papers. You make sure the Pony Express doesn't get through.

ARNOLD. I will—but I'm working on a, hee-hee, scenario of my own for tender Roady.

AVARICIA. Let's go, Debit. *(She starts to exit, but DEBIT is still flirting—with everybody.)* DEBIT!

(ALL VILLAINS exit. CHIP and PATTY re-enter, each with a brimming basket, the contents of which, mercifully, do not show.)

PATTY *(entering)*. You're right, Chip. The names of my perfumes should be tied to our life in Plop.

CHIP. Sure.

PATTY. Horsy titles, maybe. *(Brainstorming.)* For Women—*(With attitude.)* "Eau De Appaloosa" and "Parfum PinTEAU" *(Pronounced pin-TOH.)*

CHIP. How about "Musk—for Mares"?

PATTY *(nods, then:)*. On the men's side—"Gelding's Gasp."

CHIP. And—"Quarter Horse—ALL Man."

PATTY. We'll make zillions. *(A very loud, very strange SOUND, like a wet tire tube being repeatedly slapped against a wooden plank, is heard approaching, outside the door. Playwright's Note: There is an excellent sound effect hint in that last sentence.)* What's that noise?

(VANCE LANCELOT sweeps nobly in the L door.)

VANCE. That noise…is I! Vance Lancelot! *(There should be cheering for the hero. Regardless, use the next line.)*

C.B. Cheering, people! Enthusiasm, fireworks! *(When the cheering has died down, when VANCE has signed autographs, accepted kisses, whatever, action continues.)*

VANCE. Actually, the noise you heard is my mount.

(SPUD, something in the relative nature of a human being, enters, carrying the world's scroungiest saddle bags or a filthy ruck sack.)

CHIP *(peering closely at SPUD)*. This is the ugliest horse I've ever seen.

VANCE. No, no. That's my partner, Spud.

CHIP. This is the ugliest partner I've ever seen. *(SPUD makes a kind of grunt which might be loosely interpreted as, "Who asked you?")*

VANCE *(standing by the door, pointing out)*. THAT is my mount. *(PATTY and CHIP look out the doorway.)*

CHIP. What in thunder IS it?

VANCE. My loyal dolphin—Fligger.

PATTY. Roady, come look. You're not gonna believe this.

CHIP *(to VANCE)*. You rode here…on a dolphin?

VANCE. Indeed.

(ROADY enters.)

ROADY *(crossing toward SPUD, studying him... her... it).* You're right, Ma. I don't believe it. *(Arrives near SPUD.)* I can't even identify it.

PATTY. No. *(Gesturing for her to go out.)* Outside. *(ROADY and PATTY exit out front door.)*

CHIP *(turning to VANCE).* You have to keep dolphins wet, don't you? How do you manage that in the desert? *(SPUD whips a water pistol out of his saddle bag and squirts CHIP square in the face. Puts pistol away.)* Ah.

(PATTY re-enters, alone.)

PATTY. Don't you have to keep those things wet? *(SPUD squirts her, places gun back in bag.)*

VANCE *(turning to audience).* Any more questions about the dolphin's moisture level? *(There probably will be none—but if there are—SPUD moves, apparently to squirt the questioners, but he whirls at the last second and squirts CHIP. Playwright's Disclaimer: Friends and well-known good sports in the audience may be personally squirted if you want to chance it—but you'd better leave strangers alone.)*

(ROADY re-enters.)

ROADY. What a beautiful animal. *(SOUND of a dolphin's squeaking voice from off.)*

VANCE. He seems to care for you, too. But *(Smile gleaming.)* how could any male resist the charms of sweet Roady?

ARNOLD *(peeks from museum door. Aside to audience, jealously).* What have we here?

PATTY. Roady, I wouldn't even let you keep a guppy. You can forget THIS fish.

ROADY. Fligger's not a fish, Ma. He's a mammal. *(DOLPHIN replies affirmatively.)*

VANCE. I named him after two of my favorite animal heroes.

ROADY *(understanding, nodding)*. Flipper and Trigger.

VANCE. No—Ger and Flig. Who are Flipper and Trigger?

ROADY. Never mind.

(ARNOLD enters, obviously derisive of VANCE.)

ARNOLD. I don't believe I've had the pleasure.

VANCE. Maybe you should get out more.

PATTY. He means you two haven't met. Vance, this is Arnold Benedict, curator of the Poopera House.

VANCE *(extends his hand, thinks better of it, and waves instead)*. Howdy. Vance Lancelot.

ARNOLD *(obviously not)*. Charmed.

VANCE. Arnold Benedict. That name seems so familiar. Have we met before, sir?

ARNOLD. I doubt it. I HAVE certain standards. If you'll excuse me? *(Starts to exit.)*

VANCE. Certainly.

ARNOLD *(pausing at the Poopera House door)*. There are a few new blossoms in the Pooperetum, Roady. Would you care to sample their aroma?

ROADY. I'd love it, but I'm worried about Fligger.

ARNOLD *(feeling capitally snubbed, exiting)*. As you wish.

VANCE. What is your Fligger concern, sweet Roady?

C.B. *(sensing the worst)*. Oh, oh.

ROADY *(the pay-off)*. Aren't you afraid he'll dry out? *(SPUD is quick, but VANCE is quicker. He jumps between squirter and squirtee and takes the, uh, water bullet for ROADY.)*

[OPTIONAL BLOCKING SECTION] *(Before SPUD can squirt VANCE, C.B. yells...)*

C.B. CUT! *(He moves out into the audience.)* Casting call. *(Picks a MALE AUDIENCE MEMBER and brings him to the stage.)* Congratulations! You have been cast as Vance's stunt double! *(Moves VANCE from in front of ROADY, places the STUNT DOUBLE in his place, gets VANCE's hat and puts it on the DOUBLE.)* And ACTION!

ROADY *(repeating the line).* Aren't you afraid he'll dry out? *(The DOUBLE takes the squirt of water.)*

C.B. Cut! *(Escorting the DOUBLE back to the audience.)* Lovely job, just lovely! *(To STAGE.)* And ACTION! *(VANCE jumps back in place.)*

[END OPTIONAL BLOCKING SECTION]

ROADY *(reacting to VANCE).* My hero!

CHIP. Because of a squirt of water?

ROADY *(jerking CHIP aside, stage whisper).* Butt out, Pa. I WANT this guy—

CHIP. Our hero!

ARNOLD *(from doorway, aside to audience).* Curses!

VANCE. It was nothing.

PATTY. I'll say. *(ROADY gives her a swift kick in the rump.)* I'll say it was the bravest thing I ever saw.

VANCE. Old Fligger can do tricks, too. Watch. *(VANCE, CHIP, PATTY, and ROADY crowd around the door, their heads and bodies following the "action" for the audience.)* Up, big fellah. *(All "watch" the dolphin rise up.)* Roll over. *(Watch.)* Play dead. *(SOUND of one wet tire flop.)* Beg! *(One dolphin fin or a reasonable facsimile appears in the doorway. CHIP puts a nickel on it. Fin disappears.)* Spud! Prop! *(SPUD hands him a small hoop, then stands, hands inclined toward the action like Vanna White pointing to a prize.)* Through here, boy! *(Holds hoop outside and above the level of the door. CAST "watches" Fligger go up, across, and down—SOUND of a huge splash which throws a little water through the door. VANCE returns the hoop to SPUD who re-vegetates. VANCE calls to Fligger.)* High fin! *(Fin appears from side of door where Fligger flopped. VANCE and Fligger "high-five.")* I'll let him rest in that horse trough awhile.

ROADY. He's wonderful! As wonderful as—his master.

VANCE *(shyly, "Aw, shucks"-ing his feelings).* Uh, time to groom the Fligster, Spud. *(SPUD pulls a gas-station type car-window squeegee from his saddle bags, displays it to the audience, and exits. VANCE and ROADY stare at each other, transfixed.)*

ARNOLD *(aside, to audience).* O hideous circumstance! She is beginning to care for him. And he for her. And each of them for the other. And the other for each other. In short—they are—them! I will thwart this interloper and protect my sweet Roady from his unworthy attentions *(With French accent.)* "immediatement"! *(For the duller audience members:)* That means right away. It's French. You know, like the fries?

C.B. They know, they know! *(ARNOLD starts to disappear into the museum, but is distracted by the SOUND of Bach Organ music coming from beneath the trapdoor in the front desk. ARNOLD watches from the shadows. ALL look around for the source of the music. PATTY opens the desktop trapdoor and finds the source. She looks down as the music stops and a voice with an outrageous French accent is heard.)*

VOICE. Madame—what province of France is this?

PATTY. France?—this is Texas. [OPTIONAL LINE] By the way, that's a nice organ you've got there.

VOICE. Texas! *Sacre bleu! (Starts to leave.)* I must keep rowing.

PATTY. Wait! *(PATTY reaches toward him. She comes up with a white "Phantom" stylized half-mask as we hear the organ music fade away. Patty looks quizzically at the mask, then at the audience. ARNOLD exits, evilly inspired. PATTY throws the mask under the front desk as:)*

CHIP. Who was that?

PATTY. Another one of those pesky traveling organists. *(The more-or-less mainstream conversation picks up again.)*

CHIP *(to VANCE)*. So. What brings you to Plop, Vance?

VANCE *(obviously, and I mean obviously lying)*. Well, uh, it just seemed like a, uh, nice place to, uh, stop.

ROADY. I'll bet you REALLY came here on some highly-exciting, highly-*romantic* mission.

VANCE *(poorly disguising the fact that she has hit upon the truth)*. No, no, no. Just, uh, passing—through.

ROADY. A virile, *(She stops, and inhales rather heavily.)* manly-scented man like you must have many—consuming—*(One more breath.)* passions.

PATTY. Let's wait outside, Chip.

CHIP. We don't even have cable TV and you want to miss this? Sit down. *(They move out of the focus, but continue to watch.)*

VANCE *(oblivious to her lust. And most other things)*. Passions? Hmm. Well, there's my passion for fairness, of course.

ROADY *(huskily)*. And?

VANCE. Straight dealing.

ROADY *(huskily-er)*. And...for love?

VANCE. Definitely.

ROADY *(breathily)*. I knew it! [OPTIONAL] *(SPUD gives her several squirts.)*

VANCE *(very innocently—disappointing ROADY)*. There's my love for my mommy. And apple pie. And the flag. And the Fligmeister, of course.

ROADY *(deflated)*. Of course.

VANCE. But I have hatreds, as well.

ROADY *(slightly encouraged)*. Oh?

VANCE. Hatred for three things—Evil—and Dirty Dealing—and tuna.

CHIP. Tuna?!

VANCE. My Fligger lost his mate in a, uh, net-related incident a while back. *(FLIGGER sobs from offstage.)* Steady, big fellah. *(Intimately.)* I'll never forget it. A week later, I found him in the seafood aisle at Safeway, tossing little can after little can over his shoulder, squeaking, "Harriet! Are you in there?"

CHIP *(sobbing)*. Is that true?

VANCE. Yes.

CHIP. Dolphins have shoulders?

PATTY. Roady, why don't you fetch Mr. Lancelot a cup of your famous wagon-rut coffee?

ROADY. Ma, you embarrass me.

VANCE. No, thanks, Roady. I "Just Say No" to caffeine. I COULD use a spot of carp, though.

ROADY. Carp?

VANCE *(gesturing to outside)*. For—you know.

ROADY *(exiting)*. I'll check in the 'fridge. *(She exits through the museum door. All ONSTAGE CAST members look at the audience and mouth, "'Fridge?" then shrug it off.)*

CHIP *(discussing his passion)*. Vance, you've shown us your treasure, but we haven't shared ours—the Taj Mahal of Meadow-Memorabilia—the Poopera House!

VANCE *(as all exeunt into the museum)*. Are there many such collections?

CHIP. No. Go figure. *(They are gone.)*

C.B. Get ready, campers—prepare yourself for—SPECIAL EFFECTS! *(Gesturing.)* This entire room—which used to be the outside of Avaricia's office—through that door—is now the INSIDE of Avaricia's office—through that door. And all of you are Vendetta Savings and Loan employees. *(To himself.)* C.B., you are a creative genius. *(To audience members, waving sheets of paper.)* Casting best-dressed extras! Who's ready for a major career boost? *(Hands the paper to him/her. C.B. does a certain amount of "ad libbing," pointing to the proper lines and cues on pre-printed "sides," explaining, etc., in character, on each such occasion during the show.)* Listen for your cue. *(Handing another paper to another audience member.)* Here—you read this one. *(Another audience member.)* This is yours. Projection, everyone! Extra points for loudness.

(AVARICIA sweeps in, with DEBIT.)

DEBIT. Didn't that door used to open the other way?

AVARICIA. It's a stage device.

DEBIT. It sure LOOKS like a door.

AVARICIA. Come on—I've got to make sure these drudges are staying busy. *(To various audience members.)* Did you foreclose on that orphanage this morning? *(C.B. physically cues each speaker. If a line is fluffed, he "CUT"s and coaches the problem. All is handled lightheartedly, naturally.)*

BEST DRESSED EXTRA #1. It's Christmas, Miss Slime!

AVARICIA. I don't care! Throw them out! *(Laughs with deep satisfaction.)*

BEST DRESSED EXTRA #2. Even Mother Theresa?

AVARICIA. Everybody! Whiny welfare sponges!

BEST DRESSED EXTRA #3 *(holding up a glass or cup or bowl—whatever's handy).* Miss Slime—may we have more gruel?

AVARICIA. No! Get back to work!

C.B. *(if necessary).* Booing! Hissing! *(She is roundly booed, hissed, and popcorned.)*

AVARICIA *(to entire audience, all employees).* That's it, you ungrateful slug slime! I was going to raise everybody's salary to a dollar a month, but forget it. Waikiki is OUT for you this summer. *(Evil laugh.)*

DEBIT. You are so evil, Miss Avaricia.

AVARICIA *(flattered).* Please, Debit, you'll make my head swell.

DEBIT. My head was swelled once. They thought I'd have brain damage, but I guess I proved...uh...

AVARICIA. What?

DEBIT. What what?

AVARICIA. What about the brain damage?

DEBIT. No, thanks. I already ate.

(ARNOLD has sneaked into the scene. He is nearby, partly hidden by audience chairs or tables or audience members.)

ARNOLD. Avaricia! Hsssst!

DEBIT. Snake! *(DEBIT beats ARNOLD with her hat repeatedly, but slows down when AVARICIA taps on her back. DEBIT turns to AVARICIA, hands her the hat, then deliberately and visibly pulls a hair out of her own nose. AVARICIA returns the hat. DEBIT speaks to ARNOLD.)* It's called perversion therapy.

AVARICIA *(to ARNOLD).* What are you doing here? You're supposed to be watching for mailmen.

ARNOLD. Some guy's sniffing around at Chip and Patty's.

AVARICIA. He'll regret that.

ARNOLD. Please! More respect for the fertile arts.

AVARICIA. Yeah, right. So, what is this sniffer? A cowboy?

ARNOLD *(shaking his head)*. No. He's a *(Seeking the right words.)*...dolphin boy.

AVARICIA. You've gotta quit inhaling so deep in that museum.

ARNOLD. And he's set his heart on my darling Roady. And she on him. And they on...

AVARICIA. I get it.

DEBIT *(back into the conversation)*. Don't worry, Arnold. Mixed marriages never work.

ARNOLD. Mixed marriages?

DEBIT. Girls and dolphins.

ARNOLD. He's NOT a dolphin. He RIDES a dolphin. *(DEBIT just looks at him with a vacant smile—her only kind. ARNOLD turns away, stunned once again by her stupidity.)*

AVARICIA *(skeptical)*. He rides a dolphin out here in the desert?

ARNOLD. Yes.

AVARICIA. Don't you have to keep those things wet?

(SPUD pops up from the trapdoor in the desktop, gives AVARICIA a quick squirt, then pops back out.)

ARNOLD. We've got to stop wasting time. *(He rushes directly through the museum door.)*

AVARICIA *(to audience)*. You people keep working or, when I get back, everybody's going to change their underwear—with everybody else! *(She laughs her terrible, evil laugh and pushes DEBIT out the outside door—the stage device one. DEBIT steps back on, to wave sexily to C.B.)*

DEBIT *(a stage whisper).* Did I do good, Ceezy-beezy? *(AVARICIA's hand reaches through the door and drags her out again.)*

C.B. *(to audience, ignoring DEBIT).* "SPECIAL EFFECTS II." *(Waving his arms like a wizard.)* The whole room is back the way it was. *(To someone seated nearby.)* Is absolute power wonderful or what?

(CHIP, PATTY, and VANCE re-enter, the unmistakable ambiance of the museum still clinging to them.)

VANCE. That is one great museum, Chip.

CHIP. Thanks.

VANCE. Especially the Equestrian section. Every breed of horse is represented.

CHIP. Every single breed.

VANCE. Do you know what you have here?

CHIP. What?

VANCE. The best little horse house in Texas. *(There is a knock on the trapdoor in the front desk.)*

PATTY. Excuse me. *(She opens the trapdoor. A furry, PARVO-like arm hands a trophy to her from within. She reads the trophy inscription aloud.)* "Awarded to HORSE-SCENTS, for reaching the farthest possible distance to make a lame joke."

CHIP *(back to his plot line).* These rooms hold my entire life, Vance. Foofoo—and food. Food and foofoo.

VANCE. Does it ever cause any problems, working with such different things?

CHIP. Oh, I always wear gloves.

VANCE And you change them when you switch from one to the other.

CHIP. No, why?

(During the following lines, while PATTY, CHIP, and VANCE are involved in their conversation, ROADY, her hands held behind her and her mouth covered, is swept through the lobby by the love-crazed ARNOLD. He is disguised—wearing a stylized half-face mask. Rather than the traditional white, however, the mask is brown—and mottled. OK, the mask appears to be formed from a cow chip. ARNOLD takes ROADY down through the desktop trapdoor.)

PATTY. Actually, mixing up the food and the 'foo got Chip's chef career moving. Talk about your delicious accidents. What'd you call that first dish, Chip?

CHIP. "Manure Marinara."

PATTY. And the second one?

CHIP. "Primavera PooPOO."

PATTY. Then, just when business was looking up, the town started going broke. Now there's nothing for anybody to do.

[OPTIONAL SECTION] (Use this vignette if the joke means anything to your local audience—in Texas, it works.)

CHIP. Everyone's been out to see the Prairie Art a million times.

VANCE. Prairie art?

CHIP. In the marsh west of town, there's ten buckboards buried halfway to their rear axles.

VANCE. Just buckboards? No livestock?

CHIP. They couldn't manage any livestock. That was the year of the awful—cattle lack. *(Pause. The trapdoor opens and another trophy is handed out. No comment is made.)*

[END OF OPTIONAL SECTION]

CHIP. The boredom affects the women most.

VANCE. Maybe they should try quilting bees.

PATTY. We did, but it drives the bees CRAZY.

CHIP. I don't see how things could get any worse.

(AVARICIA and DEBIT burst on from AVARICIA's office.)

AVARICIA. I know a way they could get worse, Chip of my block.

CHIP. Avaricia Slime!

PATTY. And Deadbeat.

DEBIT. That's Debit!

AVARICIA. No, she may have something there.

CHIP. What do you want?

AVARICIA. Let's see. I'll have a bottle of perfume, a couple of rooms, a ten-year Poopera Pass—AND EVERYTHING ELSE!

PATTY. You don't mean...?!

AVARICIA. Yes! *(Displaying eviction notice.)* You are to be evicted for non-payment of your mortgage loan. You have three days—and get thee out.

CHIP. We paid every installment!

PATTY. We have receipts!

AVARICIA. Who signed them?

PATTY. You did!

AVARICIA. You think I'd honor the signature of a scum-scratcher like myself? Besides, you missed your payments this month AND last month!

DEBIT. I believe that you are incorrect, Miss Avaricia. *(Suddenly, inexplicably intelligent.)* While I was auditing Vendetta Savings and Loan's financial transactions for this quarter, I noted that neither Chip's nor Patty's accounts were even slightly in arrears. *(AVARICIA places her nose-hair-pinching fingernails within an inch of DEBIT's nos-*

trils. DEBIT drops back into character instantly.) Like I said, they ain't paid us nothin'!

AVARICIA *(to CHIP and PATTY)*. Carton your colognes and package your perfumes, Patty. Then vamoose. *(Sidling over to CHIP—some serious, seductive sidling.)* Chip, however, has other—very attractive—options. A simple businessgirl like myself needs a man around to—*(Seductively.)* balance her books. And Chip—you—are—my—man! *(She kind of half-snarls at him.)*

CHIP. Never!

AVARICIA. How about—*(Filthily.)* once in a while? *(CHIP considers that one until PATTY elbows him.)*

VANCE. Are you certain you have the legal right to pursue this foreclosure, madam?

AVARICIA. Who are YOU—the guy that's riding that salmon outside? *(FLIGGER makes a horrified, insulted sound.)*

VANCE *(taking umbrage)*. That is a very fishist remark, my good woman.

DEBIT. *Good woman*?! You don't know ANYTHING about her, do you?

AVARICIA *(to DEBIT)*. How'd you like your head swollen again?

DEBIT. I don't remember.

VANCE. Before anyone gets evicted, we shall pursue every legitimate means to disprove your allegations.

AVARICIA. Meaning?

PATTY. We plan to kick your legal hiney!

AVARICIA. Take it up with the District Attorney.

VANCE. Who is that?

AVARICIA. Me! Ha, ha, ha, ha! *(Etc.)* Come on, Debit! *(They exit evilly amidst thundering boos and hisses, one would earnestly hope. DEBIT's hand waves to C.B. from the doorway, then is dragged out by AVARICIA's hand.)*

C.B. Boo, boo, boo! *(To AVARICIA.)* You evil...witch! *(To audience.)* I get SO wrapped up in these things!

PATTY. Chip, whatever are we to do?

CHIP. I don't know, Patty. But, at least, things couldn't get any worse.

(The trapdoor on the front desk flies open and PARVO leaps out, yipping and yapping. The dog crosses excitedly to VANCE, CHIP and PATTY.)

PATTY. What's wrong, Parvo?

PARVO. Yip, yip, yip! Yap, yow, yow. *(Playwright's Note: I don't know what I'm writing here—the dog is barking excitedly, OK?)*

CHIP. What is it? *(Pointedly.)* Is Timmy in trouble?

PATTY. Or Jeff! Is Jeff in trouble? Or Grandpa?

VANCE. Or that stupid Forest Ranger? Is it him?

CHIP *(to VANCE)*. I hated those Forest Ranger episodes. Didn't you, Patty?

PATTY. *Hated* them. *(PARVO stops yapping and just sits there, looking at them like they've completely lost their minds.)*

C.B. Extras! *(Grabs several sheets of paper and starts handing them out to members of the audience.)* Watch for your cues, everybody—stand tall and blurt those words out. *(Speaking toward STAGE.)* ACTION!

PATTY *(resuming onstage action)*. How will we ever understand what Parvo is trying to tell us?

VANCE. We need an interpreter who can speak "Dog." *(SPUD leaps forward.)* We need an interpreter who can speak "Dog" AND "Human." *(SPUD leaps back.)*

PATTY. All is lost! *(C.B. physically cues each audience speaker.)*

AUDIENCE MEMBER. "Chip, I can speak Chihuahua."

CHIP *(looking closely at PARVO)*. Nope—too much hair.

ANOTHER AUDIENCE MEMBER. "Spitz."

CHIP. You do and you'll clean it up.

FINAL AUDIENCE MEMBER. "I am fluent in both Mutt and Cur."

VANCE. Step to the stage, young lady/man. *(If FINAL AUDIENCE MEMBER won't come, C.B. hands the paper off to somebody else. If nobody will do it, C.B. covers the part. This will probably never happen.)*

CHIP *(to PARVO)*. Tell it to her/him, boy.

PARVO *(to FINAL AUDIENCE MEMBER)*. Yip, yip, etc.

FINAL AUDIENCE MEMBER *(interpreting)*. "Sweet Roady has been abducted!"

C.B. [OPTIONAL LINE—use only if needed] Louder, sweetie, this ain't no mime troupe!

PATTY. Roady abducted? Oh, no!

VANCE. What else, Parv?

PARVO. Yip, etc.

FINAL AUDIENCE MEMBER. "She has been taken down the old well beneath the front desk!"

PATTY. The old abandoned well!

PARVO. Yap, etc.

FINAL AUDIENCE MEMBER. "Down into the aquifer!"

CHIP. Down into the…the what?

VANCE. The aquifer! Where our water—the very elixir of life—flows, deep underground!

PARVO. Yip, etc.

FINAL AUDIENCE MEMBER. "Her abductor is—the Phantom."

PATTY. The Phantom?

VANCE. Who—oh who—can this villain be?

PARVO. Yip, yip, etc.

FINAL AUDIENCE MEMBER. "One final word. I refuse to play this tick-infested flea preserve one more second." *(PARVO walks directly to C.B.'s director's chair, "lifts his leg" toward it, then storms off.)*

PATTY. Parvo, come home!

C.B. Forget him. *(Crossing to the FINAL AUDIENCE MEMBER.)* Splendid job! Splendid! *(Ushering FINAL AUDIENCE MEMBER from the stage to her/his chair.)* My people will call your people. *(He walks away. Calls.)* Toad! That final audience member? She(He) NEVER works in this town again. *(Mumbled indecipherable cursing from offstage. To STAGE.)* ACTION!

VANCE. Fear not, gentle Chip and noble Patty. Ease yourselves, gentle Patty and noble Chip. Vance Lancelot—and Spud—will unravel this mortgage business, save your worldly goods, hire MUCH better actors, and rescue sweet Roady from the bowels of the earth.

PATTY. Oh, thank you!

CHIP. How long will that take, Vance?

VANCE *(looking at his wrist)*. If watches had been invented, I'd say we could mop it up by the end of intermission. Let's ride, Spud. *(VANCE and SPUD exit.)*

CHIP. I "fear not" already.

PATTY. And I am SO eased.

(VANCE is heard, shrieking in agony. He bursts back onto the set, totally distraught.)

VANCE. Fligger...is GONE! *(VANCE falls, in a dead faint. CHIP and PATTY rush to him as stage lights go down. House lights up.)*

C.B. *(visibly, theatrically exhausted).* Oh! I am so wrung out! Take fifteen, people. Take fifteen. *(Calling off.)* Toad, prepare my liqueur! *(C.B. exits, grandly, of course, as TOAD's inevitable unidentifiable cursing fades.)*

END OF ACT ONE

ACT TWO

AT RISE: *The next day. C.B. moves onstage, followed by TOAD, who is still stinging from his Act One humiliations.*

C.B. In recognition of your marvelous work, I have a plum role for you in Act Two, Toad.

TOAD. Great. I'm playing a plum.

C.B. *(handing him script pages).* No, no—here are your pages.

TOAD. Which charac…

C.B. Scoot along. Wardrobe has the information. *(Calling to others as TOAD exits.)* Act Two, people! And…ACTION!

(VANCE is stretched out, the front desk serving as his sick-bed. Naturally, he is delirious. PATTY is near him.)

VANCE *(deliriously).* Fligger! I'm on my way. Daddy will rescue you. *("Runs" in his sleep, thrashing his legs.)*

PATTY. We must help poor Vance.

CHIP. Poor Vance!? How about us? In two days, we've got no more home than a dolphin. *(From his coma, VANCE moans in agony.)* And there's the tiny matter of a missing daughter.

PATTY. We must think first of others. I have summoned the mystic healer.

CHIP. Not that bozo, Woman-Who-Fixes-Ow-Ows?

PATTY. More reverence for the healer, please.

(TOAD appears, dressed as an extremely ancient, very cheesy, "Healer" woman.)

TOAD *(to C.B.)*. I'll get you for this, C.B.

PATTY. Woman-Who-Fixes-Ow-Ows, you honor our home.

WOMAN. Yeah, yeah. *(Looking at VANCE.)* Is this the wimp who's whining for his fish?

PATTY *(nodding)*. How may we restore his mind and spirit?

WOMAN *(finally accepting the role)*. There are many traditional remedies. *(Jewish schtick.)* You've tried already chicken soup?

PATTY. Yes.

WOMAN *(dropping Jewish character)*. Perhaps a necklace of live fire ants.

CHIP. How does the necklace stay together?

WOMAN. I make the ants hold hands.

PATTY. Ah.

WOMAN. There is one other therapy which sometimes succeeds.

PATTY. Try it.

WOMAN *(moves to U of VANCE, looks to the skies, raises her hands upward, chants a bit, leans toward the fevered face and shrieks)*. Wake up, stupid! *(Of course, VANCE awakens immediately.)*

CHIP. Why didn't we think of that?

PATTY. She's a trained professional.

WOMAN *(exiting toward C.B.)*. I go, to pray over a corpse.

CHIP. Who died?

WOMAN. No one. Yet. *(Approaching C.B.)*

C.B. Haven't you heard of suffering for your art?

TOAD *(removing WOMAN-garb)*. Get ready to experience it.

C.B. *(putting his arm around TOAD).* This can all be settled so easily—over a drink, maybe. *(He ushers the fuming TOAD out as focus shifts back to the stage.)*

VANCE *(coming around).* Aunty Em, there was a scarecrow and a tin woods—Wait a minute. I'm in Plop, aren't I?

CHIP. In EVERY sense of the word.

VANCE *(remembering).* Is Fligger all right?

PATTY. We...haven't heard.

VANCE *(overacting—even for him).* Depths of despair! Anguish and agony! And what of sweet Roady?

PATTY. Still missing.

VANCE *(dropping to minor concern).* Dang.

PATTY. Spud's investigating.

CHIP. Have you ever noticed that Spud is...just a little weird?

VANCE. It's not his fault. He was abandoned by his parents when he was very young.

PATTY. How young?

VANCE. Well, as soon as they saw him. He'd have died if it weren't for a family of prairie dogs.

PATTY. Spud was raised by prairie dogs?

VANCE. Just until things got tight in the burrow. Then it was foster home after foster home.

PATTY. Tragic.

VANCE. He even bunked with a family of potatoes for a time. They were the ones who named him. He had their mother's eyes.

CHIP. You expect us to believe a half-baked story like that?

PATTY. Chip!

VANCE. I'm not sure where all he stayed after that, but, once in a while, a few unusual behaviors kick in.

PATTY. Like?

VANCE. Like—if he asks you to go for a walk in the moonlight—don't. Or if you find him hanging upside down by his toes and making high-pitched noises—smile. *(Footsteps, or something, approach.)* Shh, I think I hear him.

CHIP *(trying to get on his good side)*. Spud, your shirt's kind of worn. *(Indicating his own shirt.)* Could I offer you this one? *(SPUD makes a decidedly negative sound. CHIP backs away.)*

VANCE. Spud doesn't like that kind of collar.

CHIP. What kind of collar does he like?

VANCE. Flea and tick. Tell me everything you found out, Spud. *(SPUD stands perfectly still, his expression unchanged.)* I was afraid of that.

CHIP. Let's all grab a cup of wagon-track java, work on a plan, and yield focus to the next scene.

(VANCE, CHIP and ROADY exit, just before C.B. and TOAD re-enter, TOAD encased in the PARVO suit again. What an idiot.)

TOAD. You're SURE there was fan mail about my Parvo portrayal?

C.B. Have I ever lied to you?

TOAD. Only when your lips were moving.

C.B. See? I'm WAY overdue to tell the truth. So rush into that museum and lend a...paw to these people.

TOAD *(crossing into the Poopera House, to himself)*. I can't believe you're doing this again, Toad. *(Hitting himself on the head with a rolled newspaper.)* BAD DOG! BAD DOG! *(He disappears as C.B. speaks.)*

C.B. "SPECIAL EFFECTS III—THE SEARCH FOR CHEAPER AND CHEAPER SHOOTING LOCATIONS." We journey, deep beneath the earth, to the aquifer. You know, where the water is. I transform this murky spot into—that murky spot. *(To nearby audience member.)* Who says you need big budgets to create art? *(Waves his hand, wand-like, toward ARNOLD's entrance.)*

(Lights fade out onstage and come up in the audience, a kind of putrid shade of green, to suggest the underwater caverns. From somewhere at the periphery of the audience, ARNOLD, wearing his cow-chip mask, a wide-brimmed dress hat and, perhaps, a cape, drifts on. ROADY is with him, his prisoner. He has a long stick and seems to be "poling" them through the water. Rather than traveling in a boat, however, each wears a cheap little-kid's swimming pool plastic inner tube, complete with ducky or doggy heads—and they are obviously walking. ROADY's hands are bound and her inner tube is linked to his with a chain or rope. ARNOLD and, to a degree, ROADY, take this "phantom" device seriously even though, surely, the audience will not.)

ROADY. When am I to be released from your terrible clutches, Mister...*(Tiring of the charade already.)* Oh, Arnold, will you drop this stupid mask routine?

ARNOLD *(poling)*. Arnold? I am known as "The Phantom."

ROADY. Known by whom?

ARNOLD. Everyone has heard of—"The Phantom of the Poopera"?

ROADY *(sarcastically)*. Oh, THAT phantom. Yeah, everybody knows "The Phantom of the Poopera." I'm surprised you aren't being mobbed by women crying to bear your children.

ARNOLD. Sarcasm is a blotch on your innocence.

ROADY. Arnie—your face smells.

ARNOLD *(nearing an exit)*. They're not making heroines like they used to.

C.B. *(calling)*. Choir! Two notes! *(Several audience members who were recruited during the intermission to form the SHARK CHOIR, are heard. C.B. conducts ALL choir notes.)*

SHARK CHOIR *(a long low note, followed by a shorter, higher note)*. Bahhhhh—duuumm.

ARNOLD *(poling them through the exit)*. What—was that? *(They are gone.)*

C.B. Lovely foreshadowing. Scene shift!

(VANCE, PATTY, and CHIP return to the stage. Stage lights up. Audience lights out.)

VANCE *(entering. To CHIP and PATTY)*. Did you call her "Roady" after that old song, "Go Tell Aunt Rhody"?

PATTY. No, it's short for...you don't want to know.

CHIP *(nearly breaking down)*. Oh, my sweet baby! I'm so worried.

VANCE. That she might be—harmed?

CHIP. No. That she'll kill the guy. Then guess who gets the undertaker's bill?!

(AVARICIA and DEBIT burst on from AVARICIA's office door.)

AVARICIA. Only two days to paradise, my rippling Chip. *(Looking around the audience.)* Boy, it smells like a damp aquifer in here.

DEBIT. Stage device. *(To C.B.)* Right, oogie-boogie?

C.B. Shhh.

AVARICIA *(to CHIP)*. Give us a big kiss, firelips.

CHIP. Yeeeecccchhh!

AVARICIA. Ah—playing hard-to-get.

CHIP. I ain't playing.

AVARICIA. Your taunts only feed my…lust.

DEBIT *(patting AVARICIA's rump).* SOMETHIN'S sure been feedin' you. *(With the speed of a gazelle, if not the grace, she leaps at DEBIT's nose and yanks out some hairs.)*

AVARICIA *(to audience).* Fastest nostril in the west.

DEBIT *(to audience, as she tends her nose).* Subversion therapy.

PATTY. We're not ready to cash in our chips, Avaricia Slime!

AVARICIA. Two days, ex-wife-to-be. *(To CHIP.)* Keep thinking about me, honey-bun. I'm heading back to the Savings and Loan now…to compound my interest. *(Starts to exit.)* And, why don't you send Spud over? His face is a great exterminator. *(Evil laugh.)*

(SPUD makes an ugly sound—what choice does he have—as AVARICIA exits. DEBIT starts to exit, but gets distracted by a handsome audience member. DEBIT is moving toward him when AVARICIA looks back in.)

AVARICIA. Debit! *(DEBIT reluctantly exits.)*

VANCE. Spud, go pretend to exterminate at Avaricia's—but your REAL task is to sniff out something we can use against that foul woman. *(SPUD, actively sniffing, very actively, exits.)*

(PARVO wanders on, to a couch.)

CHIP. What good can Spud do against the cunning of Avaricia Slime?

VANCE. Don't underestimate him. The months he spent with his foster family of bloodhounds were some of his dearest. And it's where he learned about personal grooming. *(Back on the track.)* But enough chit-chat. I go—to rescue the love and passion of my life. I'll keep an eye out for Roady, too.

CHIP. But you don't know the territory.

VANCE. True. I need—a native tracker. *(All turn, as one—and look at PARVO, who has been sitting on a couch, idly scratching. He senses their gaze, looks up—and speaks—in perfect human English, if a bit "cartoony-doggy.")*

PARVO *(shaking his head)*. Uh, uh. This pup ain't goin' no place.

CHIP. Parvo can speak!

VANCE. How came this miracle to pass?

C.B. *(to audience)*. Tell 'em, extras. *(To STAGE.)* It's a…

ALL AUDIENCE MEMBERS *(PARVO holds up large cue card for them to read, on which is written:)* Stage device!

VANCE. Parvo, you must help us. If not for me—for the town—for the family.

PARVO. No.

VANCE. For animal rights—for animal lefts!

PARVO. Can't help you.

VANCE. I'll give you a doggy treat.

PARVO. Not for every kibble and every bit in the territory.

VANCE. For Spaniel Sparkies?

PARVO. Nope.

VANCE. Doggy Droolies?

PARVO. Forget it.

VANCE *(his trump card)*. A full-color…Benji…fan magazine? *(Update this gag, if needed.)*

PARVO *(pause, then lustily)*. The swimsuit issue?

VANCE. Naturally.

PARVO *(jumping up and "pointing")*. I'm your hound. *(VANCE and PARVO both rush to the front desk, open the trapdoor, and disappear—down into the aquifer.)*

CHIP *(looking down into the hole)*. You boys be careful.

PATTY. Let's drown our sorrows in a cup of sweet Roady's Cappuccino Ca-Ca-Ca. *(Rhythm: Cha-Cha-Cha.)*

[OPTIONAL JOKE—Mature—if stupid—material]
CHIP. More coffee? I'm gonna be up all night.
PATTY *(as they exit).* I've heard that one before.
[END OF OPTIONAL JOKE]

C.B. *(as CHIP and PATTY exit).* Cross-fade—to the aquifer! *(To audience.)* I get to say such nifty words.

(ARNOLD and ROADY enter from whence they exited, he still poling. Lights switch to the green audience setting.)

ARNOLD. So—have you come to love me yet, my prairie poppy?

ROADY. During two lobby scenes and a low-budget ducky ride? You must be on drugs.

ARNOLD. Eventually, you shall accept my charms.

ROADY. Right. Just after you pole us fast enough to water ski.

C.B. Choir! *(The previously-recruited and intermission-coached SHARK CHOIR begins its number. C.B. holds up cue card.)*

SHARK CHOIR. Baaaahhh—dummm.

ARNOLD. That noise again. What is it?

ROADY. Sounds like something going *(Repeating the sound.)* Baaah—dumm.

ARNOLD. I know that. But what IS it?

C.B. Two more notes!

SHARK CHOIR. Baaahhh—dummm.

ARNOLD *(realizing).* Oh, my lord!

C.B. Again!

SHARK CHOIR. Baaaahhh—dummm!

ARNOLD. Shark! *(ARNOLD starts to pole feverishly. ROADY and ARNOLD "float" all around the audience area, moving more and more quickly, as if followed by a predator. The CHORUS number is performed in its entirety this time.)*

C.B. *(prepared for the downbeat).* Full number, my little chorines—Spanish version!

SHARK CHOIR. Baaaah-dummm! Baaaah-dummm! Baah-dummm! *(The pay-off.)* Ba-duh-duh-duh-duh-da-dum. *(This last musical "phrase" is the* "Mexican Hat Dance."*)*

C.B. The attack! *(All lights go out.)*

ARNOLD. Aaaaaaaiiiiiiiieeeeeee!

ROADY *(from the darkness).* Fligger! It's you!...My hero! *(FLIGGER's high-pitched squeal, celebrating his triumph.)*

ARNOLD. Damn stupid dolphin.

(In the dark, ROADY and ARNOLD move to the stage and hide behind the front desk, as do ALL except CHIP and PATTY. Lights up onstage as CHIP and PATTY enter, still distraught.)

PATTY. Why haven't we heard anything?

CHIP. The telegraph lines are probably down...

PATTY. We don't have a telegraph.

CHIP. OK, but the lines could STILL be down!

PATTY. What does that...

(VANCE, interrupting, pops up from the front desk trap-door, trailed by PARVO, ROADY, and ARNOLD.)

VANCE. We have returned—our mission a success!

PARVO. YOUR mission? You didn't do anything.

VANCE *(shushing him, indicating CHIP and PATTY)*. THEY don't know that.

PATTY. Yes, we do. We were watching backstage.

CHIP *(whips off ARNOLD's mask)*. Arnold! I am so disappointed in you.

ARNOLD *(sarcastically)*. Boy, is THAT going to haunt my dreams.

VANCE *(wrapping ARNOLD's wrists with his ducky rope tether—or not)*. I arrest you for the abduction of sweet Roady, Arnold Benedict.

ARNOLD. How can you arrest me?

VANCE. Because my true identity is—Vance Lancelot—U.S. Marshal. AND Special Investigator for the Pony Express.

ARNOLD. I've had much better days than this.

VANCE *(to CHIP and PATTY)*. It is my pleasure to safely return your daughter.

PARVO. You? Roady dragged Arnold up here while you were still trying to find the men's room.

VANCE. Is it my fault that running water makes me…

ROADY *(rushing to cover for her man)*. But Vance came forth, boldly seeking us—in the rushing, flowing waves of the…

VANCE *(interrupting, squirming uncomfortably, crossing his legs)*. Roady…

ROADY. Sorry, my hero.

PARVO *(at the end of his rope—leash—whatever—he's totally ticked. [Think about it])*. Hero, hero, hero! How about the poochie? I never get squat! OK, I GET to squat, but that's all! More importantly, I have been criminally undercast.

VANCE. Settle down, boy.

PARVO. Wake up, will you! I'm not really a dog! I'm an actor! Everybody knows it. *(To ROADY.)* You know it, don't you?

ROADY. Hey, I've dated worse.

PARVO. I'm out of here!

VANCE. Stay, boy! Heel!

PARVO *(exiting)*. Jeesh.

ROADY. Do you know what this means?

VANCE. For one thing, it's time to call an obedience school.

CHIP. Pardon me. Has anybody given ANY thought to the foreclosure? *(A voice, very deep and resonant, is heard from the trapdoor.)*

VOICE. That issue has been resolved.

(The trapdoor opens and SPUD drags AVARICIA and DEBIT into the room.)

VANCE. You two have been very, very bad.

AVARICIA. We're villains! What'd you expect, a charity telethon?

VANCE *(gets the letters from SPUD and hands them to CHIP)*. These letters should be of interest.

CHIP *(instantly speed-reading both letters)*. The perfume deal! And my Grange-grunge Grant! They came through!

PATTY. Plop will be on the map again!

CHIP. Messy.

VANCE. Actually, I knew about your successes all along. I am also—Vance Lancelot—President of the Phoenix Fragrance Foundation AND Chairman of the National Endowment for the Fertilization Arts.

PATTY. Why didn't you tell us?

VANCE. Who'd come see a ten-minute play? Plus, my mission was to investigate wrong-doings.

CHIP. Never mind that. Who was the deep voice that said, "That issue has been resolved!" at the top of this script page? *(SPUD pulls a cassette tape player out of his saddle bags, presses a button, and the tape says, in the same resonant voice:)*

TAPED VOICE. "That issue has been resolved." *(SPUD turns the machine off.)*

CHIP. What is that thing? *(SPUD presses the button—this schtick will continue for a while.)*

TAPED VOICE. A tape recorder.

PATTY. But those haven't been inven...

AVARICIA *(grabbing CHIP, and pulling a derringer from her...shirt)*. Everybody freeze! *(The entire cast starts to shiver, as if freezing.)* Are there NO jokes too cheap for this show?

TAPED VOICE. Probably not.

AVARICIA. Never mind! Debit—you cover them...*(Thinks better of it.)* and if you pull a blanket out of someplace, I'll shoot YOU. *(DEBIT, who has been moving toward the front desk, stops and comes back.)*

VANCE *(to AVARICIA)*. What...are you going to do?

AVARICIA. My dreams of ecstasy with Chip aren't to be so easily dashed. *(To CHIP.)* Any moment, now, my manure magnate, we'll be—pooling our equities. *(Waving the derringer around.)* Everybody hide your eyes and count to one hundred. *(ALL comply, including DEBIT, who counts the loudest of all, running into trouble around "four." SPUD's tape machine can be heard counting in the midst of them.)*

DEBIT. One—two—three—*(Raising her head)* What comes after "three"?

AVARICIA. Your I.Q. *(OTHERS count lowly under this.)*

DEBIT *(covering her eyes again)*. "My I.Q.-five-six—

AVARICIA *(shrieking)*. YOU DON'T HAVE TO COUNT, DEBIT! YOU'RE COMING WITH ME!

DEBIT. Oh.

AVARICIA. Nobody move for five minutes—or ELSE! *(She sweeps CHIP out the front door—no, not with a broom. DEBIT exits as well, recovering from the counting trauma.)*

VANCE *(leaping up)*. One hundred! Ready or not, here I come! *(Starts to rush out the door.)*

PATTY. What about the five minutes?

VANCE. Who's got a watch?

ROADY *(pointing to an audience member)*. This guy does.

VANCE. What does it say?

ROADY *(looking at watch)*. "Made in Korea." Mama—my first cheap joke!

PATTY. Our little girl is finally cheap.

ARNOLD *(sarcastically)*. Keen.

VANCE. Five minutes, shmive minutes—we must save our cheerful chum, the Chipper! *(Turning to the door.)* Hi-yo, Fligger!

(VANCE rushes out the door, followed by PATTY and ROADY. ARNOLD wanders into the audience and sits, visiting with whomever, during the next bits. AVARICIA, DEBIT, and their prisoner, CHIP, have been hiding just offstage. They rush back on.)

AVARICIA. We'll hide in the aquifer—they'll never think to look there

DEBIT. Where?

AVARICIA. The aquifer!

DEBIT. Where?

C.B. Everybody! [OPTIONAL] *(Holding up a sign reading, "The Aquifer!")*

AUDIENCE. *The aquifer*!

DEBIT. Oh. Ha, ha, ha. What's an aquifer? *(AVARICIA reaches into DEBIT's nose and drags her along by a nose hair—to the trapdoor in the front desk. AVARICIA, DEBIT and CHIP exit there.)*

(VANCE re-enters with PATTY and ROADY.)

VANCE. I wonder where they could have gone?

C.B. Extras—tell him!

AUDIENCE. *The aquifer*!

VANCE. Follow me!

C.B. Scene shift! Submerged schtick in the waterous caverns!

(As the CHASERS enter the trapdoor, AVARICIA, CHIP and DEBIT come out from some doorway, "into the aquifer." The schtick now becomes underwater action and props—one, or one set, per performer—diving masks, snorkels, flappy swim fins, those inflatable flotation arm things children use, large "animal" floats, etc., etc. [In the midst of all this, PARVO will come walking through, at normal speed, still cursing unintelligibly, oblivious to everything around him—he is still really mad.] Of course, there are all varieties of swimming strokes—freestyle, butterfly, backstroke, dog paddle, and impossible variations. AVARICIA, DEBIT, and CHIP perform a lovely water ballet—a study in synchronized swimming. About then, PATTY, ROADY, SPUD, and, last of all, VANCE, enter from the doorway, also "underwater costumed," and join the chase. For locomotion, someone probably should have a paddle, someone else a large oar, someone a guitar, someone makes the sound and mimes the action of an outboard motor, etc., etc. [I'm starting to sound like Yul Bryn-

ner.] The clarity of who is chasing whom probably breaks down and I can't imagine how it could matter less. At some point, rather earlier than later—don't belabor the chase beyond the fun of it—AVARICIA and DEBIT are caught—by ROADY. VANCE is around somewhere, lending little, if any, assistance. AVARICIA is disarmed.)

C.B. Cheering! The Evil Avaricia is defeated! And CUT! *(ALL actors drop character, slog to the stage in miscellaneous ways, and carelessly take places for the next scene.)* And...ACTION! *(ALL actors immediately begin coughing, as if recovering from their underwater experience. Full character is instantly assumed.)*

VANCE *(to AVARICIA).* I finally brought you to justice, vile villainous viper!

AVARICIA. Spare me your alliteration!

CHIP. But Roady did all the work.

ROADY *(kicking him again).* Ixnay, addy-day.

CHIP. Our hero!

PATTY. Forget all that. *(She grabs ARNOLD, who has just been sitting, hands bound, waiting, bored, in the audience, though all of this, and draws him up.)* What charges do we plan to press against Arnold?

CHIP. Mail fraud, aggravating kidnapping, and some SERIOUS water pollution.

ARNOLD *(embarrassed).* That shark REALLY scared me.

PATTY. He also stole two ducky flotation devices from Sunshine Shirley's Swim-Support Center.

CHIP *(horrified).* Let's get a rope AND a tree.

ROADY. Daddy! Compassion!

CHIP *(whining).* It would perk up the whole weekend, Roady. *(ROADY shakes her head, "No," and CHIP pouts.)*

VANCE. My most important job of all hasn't even been revealed yet.

PATTY. What job?

VANCE. I am—Vance Lancelot—the mail-order bride that sweet Roady sent for.

ROADY. My bride!? Oh, ecstasy. But, we have no mail service. How did you know I wished to send for you?

VANCE. I learned it from—the Network of Psychic Friends.

ROADY. Somehow, I knew you were going to say that.

VANCE. Sadly, I will be unable to fulfill my bridely duties.

ROADY. What?

VANCE. My heart belongs—to another. *(FLIGGER's voice is heard, lovingly shrieking. VANCE, as if to say, "There is my true love now—sorry," gestures toward the sound, then crosses and holds Fligger's fin.)*

[ALTERNATE VANCE MATCHING] *(After "belongs to another," VANCE moves to an audience member, perhaps the DOG INTERPRETER or anybody, really, so long as it's a surprise and an embarrassment to the victim.)*
[END OF ALTERNATE]

ROADY *(lightning switch, trying to salvage something. Crossing to ARNOLD)*. Then I am free to accept the love of the one man whose passion…

DEBIT *(interrupting, pointing to ARNOLD)*. Look, boss! That cute Poopera guy is going to jail, too. *(To ARNOLD.)* Ya think we could be "cell-mates," Arnold?

ARNOLD *(scooting to DEBIT's side, recognizing a fabulous deal when he sees one)*. Sorry, Roady. The nights are really long up the river.

DEBIT. Especially after dark. *(To C.B., indicating ARNOLD.)* C.B., can I keep him?

C.B. With my blessing, children.

(ARNOLD gives C.B. the old "thumbs up." ROADY moves aside and sulks as another character, obviously played by TOAD, enters, carrying a briefcase.)

LAWYER. I am Plughorse Strains, lawyer representing Mr. Toad Hall. May I speak to a *(Checking notes.)* C.B. Se-Ville, please?

C.B. *(points to some innocent member of the audience)*. There's your man.

LAWYER *(moving toward the audience member)*. My client maintains that you…

C.B. *(to TOAD)*. If we might continue?

LAWYER *(to audience member)*. Don't run off after the show.

ROADY *(getting desperate, moving toward TOAD)*. At last, my true love has come back to me.

AVARICIA *(pushing ROADY aside, crossing to TOAD)*. Forget it, honey. I need a lawyer more than you do. *(To TOAD, lasciviously.)* And I really NEED one.

TOAD *(appealing to the boss, near panic)*. C.B.!

C.B. With my blessing, children. AND my permission. *(AVARICIA gives TOAD a pinch on the bottom.)*

TOAD *(jumping, grabbing his bottom)*. Stop, Avaricia!

AVARICIA. You're a lawyer, aren't ya? I'm just checking your briefs!

ROADY *(moving, in desperation, to C.B.)*. At last, my true love has…

C.B. Forget it, girly. C.B. SeVille has obligations on the coast. You want to see our family vacation pictures from the LaBrea Tar Pits?

ROADY *(dropping character, furious at C.B.)*. So who AM I going to marry? This is a melodrama, buddy, and melodramas don't just leave the heroine sitting around quilting bees.

C.B. C.B. SeVille thinks of everything. *(Gesturing.)* Spouse! *(SPUD pulls a bridal veil from his saddle bags, puts it on his head, and steps to DC, demurely awaiting ROADY. ROADY looks at him, gives a huge stage sigh, and moves to his side, gazing forced-lovingly at him, uh, it, uh... SPUD.)*

PATTY *(to CHIP)*. Look, Chip. We have a new...something-in-law.

CHIP. And we can look forward to bouncing little Grand-...whatevers.

SPUD *(pushes tape recorder button. Nothing happens. Pushes again. Still nothing. Finally speaking)*. What the hey. I love you, sweet Roady.

ROADY *(Frankenstein movie schtick)*. It's ALIVE! *(She throws her arms around SPUD. He smiles. I guess.)*

C.B. And...CUT! Print it! *(Winding things up.)* Curtain call! Extras first! House lights! *(Has EXTRAS stand in place in the audience or, in small theatres, he has them come to the stage.)* Avaricia's featured drudges...doggy interpreters...Shark Choir...C.B. SeVille's impersonator. Men Debit flirted with—no, there's too many of those. *(To those already in place.)* And...bow! *(The EXTRAS take what is surely a clumsy bow. C.B. dismisses EXTRAS.)* Thank you! Now, Cast curtain call! Chip and Patty! *(Both bow, holding their precious chip baskets.)* Arnold and Debit! *(Bow—DEBIT starts to head for an audience member, ARNOLD pulls her back.)* Vance and Fligger! *(VANCE bows, then gestures to the door. FLIGGER's fin does a "salaam" sort of bow and makes several squeaks.)* Avaricia and Toad!

(AVARICIA drags TOAD to C. He is crying.) Roady and Spud! *(Both move into place, DC. Then C.B. takes C stage himself.)* Finally, C.B. SeVille—your fabulously gifted director! *(Takes an elaborate bow. Then, to audience.)* Now—the rest of you people—

FULL CAST. Get out of here!! *(Closing music up as ALL exit.)*

THE END

PRODUCTION NOTES

SET

A sign on the U wall of the lobby reads, "CHIP AND PATTY'S ROOMING HOUSE—Plop's Prime Place to Plop." There is an entrance U and R of the front desk, U. There are two other entrances—diagonal at DL and diagonal at DR. A sign above the DR door reads, "POOPERA HOUSE this way." The DL door leads "outside." Not obvious to the audience is a "trapdoor" in the top of the front desk which also serves as an Entrance/Exit and for other stage devices. (Hidden behind the desk is an "escape" opening in the U wall through which characters may exit or enter, unseen by the audience.) There are a few crummy furniture items—in the approximate nature of any combination of chairs, couches, love seats, and/or benches. On a side stage or at the very DR edge of the set, C.B. SEVILLE's tall Director's Chair awaits his presence.

MUSIC

HORSE-SCENTS is published without music or music cues and it certainly may be presented that way. The addition of a pianist or keyboard player, however, magnifies the fun. An empathetic musician can provide evil chords for the villains, heroic chords for the, uh, hero, and dumb chords for practically everybody else. Little "quotes" from old and new tunes may bring special meaning to local audiences. The variations are limited only by the inventiveness of the keyboardist and most of the ones I've run across are inventiveness poster children. Such musical support also helps the cast and, indeed, the audience, jump into the rhythm of the piece.

COSTUMES

Cliches and stereotypes rule the day here. Virtually all costumes are Western or Melodrama "types." Here are a few suggestions:

› C.B.: Beret, silk scarf, silk shirt, puttees, riding boots
› TOAD: Whatever the actor feels "right" wearing. Requires either quick changeability or an ease of "overdressing" for several double castings. (PARVO, WOMAN-WHO-FIXES-OW-OWS.)
› CHIP: Old-time "hick." The guy's big passion is manure—what did you think he would wear?
› PATTY: Homespun or gingham dress and apron.
› ROADY: A "pretty" dress, a "pretty" hair bow, other stuff—all "pretty."
› VANCE: White cowboy hat, white cowboy shirt, white pants, white boots. Optional—white accessories.
› SPUD: The dirtiest rags anybody can find. A contest should probably be held.
› ARNOLD: Villain suit. Black coat and pants, white shirt, string tie. Spats would be nice, but they're kind of pricey. Slouch hat, cape, and mottled brown "Phantom" half-mask.
› AVARICIA: Sensuous villain look. Black outfit, boots or heels, jaunty Western hat, bright red wig, etc. Exaggerated cleavage, no matter how you come up with it, is a plus.
› DEBIT: Cute, sexy, dumb—in some order. Perhaps short-shorts, bare midriff, boots, silly cowboy hat pinned up in the front.
› PARVO: Cheap, probably ratty, full body dog costume. The actor's face must be visible. Facial expressions and reactions are crucial. A "full head" costume of the sports mascot type does not work, seriously impedes the under-

standing of PARVO's spoken lines, and is an unforgivable esthetic *faux pas.*

› WOMAN-WHO-FIXES-OW-OWS: Perhaps a sack-cloth or burlap or buckskin-look dress, headband, obviously cheap wig.
› PLUGHORSE: Lawyer outfit, whatever that is. Maybe a swallow-tail coat. No attempt is made to disguise TOAD.

PROPS

› C.B.: Riding crop or swagger stick, various sets of script pages ("sides"), tall Director's chair. (Optional: large audience cue cards.)
› TOAD: Clipboard with notes, clapboard slate, small megaphone, rolled newspaper, audience sign.
› CHIP: Large pot and wooden spoon, Easter basket, prop cow chips, swim mask, snorkel, kids' arm flotation things.
› PATTY: Perfume atomizer, Easter basket, prop cow chips, white "Phantom" half-mask, a trophy (or two), swim mask, flippers.
› ROADY: Writing paper and pen, box of letters, swim mask, snorkel.
› VANCE: None. Perfection abhors being gilded.
› SPUD: Saddlebags or ruck sack, large water pistol, small bright-colored hoop, service-station type window squeegee, swim mask, canoe paddle, LOUD battery-powered cassette tape recorder and tape, wedding veil.
› ARNOLD: Plate of prop cow chips, two "confirmation letters," mottled brown "Phantom" mask, boat-pole, two ducky swimming pool ring floats and rope tether.
› AVARICIA: Eviction notice, small "derringer" pistol (hidden in her bos…uh, shirt), swim mask, snorkel.
› DEBIT: Swim mask, snorkel, flippers (all worn incorrectly).

- FLIGGER: Fin (on a stick), deflated tire tube and large wooden plank or other FLIGGER-gallop simulator. All props are controlled by the offstage person who portrays FLIGGER.
- PLUGHORSE: Briefcase.
- AUDIENCE: Popcorn. Bad taste shields. (That's a joke.)

DIRECTOR'S NOTES

DIRECTOR'S NOTES

DIRECTOR'S NOTES

DIRECTOR'S NOTES

DIRECTOR'S NOTES